I0479359

HORSEMEN OF
THE MING DYNASTY
明代骑手

Volume 1 of Art of the Ming

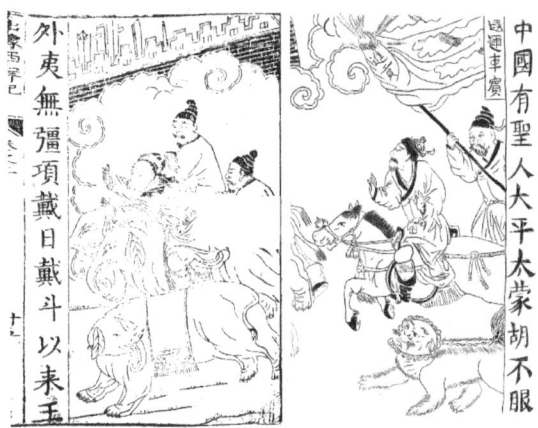

An Art Coloring Book of

Selected Restored Artwork

from

Luo Mao Deng's epic

An Account of the Western World Voyages of the San Bao Eunuch

三宝太监西洋记

Restored & Compiled & Translated
by
Laurie Bonner-Nickless
劳丽 邦纳 -- 尼克利斯

Member of the Expert's Panel for

The Silk Road Sustainable Development Institute

Copyright © 2023 Laurie Bonner-Nickless

All rights reserved.

ISBN:
ISBN-13:

DEDICATION

To the original artists whose names have been lost,
I hope I did your work justice.
To Mark, whose bright idea gave birth to this side project,
and whose patience was often tested.
And, especially to Kyle, our research assistant,
a great friend & a true wizard of all tech,
this would never have been finished if not for your help.

ACKNOWLEDGMENTS

This is a work comprised of restored illustrations from the pages of an epic work by Luo Mao Deng.
After far too long, the diligent work of his illustrators will once more be seen as it should be.

The chapter titles and picture captions were translated with the aid of several mechanical translation engines.
But, that was only the starting point.

Baidu's excellent on-line dictionaries helped us lift our understanding from a vague hope to reality.

Kyle Ames' brilliant & careful work as our research assistant cannot be overly praised.

No work of art or scholarship is ever done in a vacuum,
Without those who stand beside us, we are nothing.

TABLE OF CONTENTS

About the original book that was the source of these pictures

In 1585, Luo Maodeng began publishing a serialized epic account of the seventh and final set of voyages of the great Ming Treasure fleet. Luo titled it <u>An Account of the Western World Voyages of the San Bao Eunuch</u>. It told a story of exploits of a great Ming Admiral and Court Eunuch named Zheng He, along with that of the men and women who set sail with him.

We do not currently know exactly who Luo Mao Deng was or who was the artist or artists who illustrated that story. There are some hints that Luo may have been highly placed in the Imperial government, since he had access to the newly reopened section of the Imperial archives that had been sealed for one hundred and fifty years since soon after the final return of the great fleet to its home port. There is far clearer evidence that the same artists worked on the illustrations for another epic set of adventures, <u>The Journey West</u>, the first publication of the much beloved folk tales describing the mischievous antics and grand adventures of the Monkey King and his companions.

It has long been debated by some about how much of Luo's account is fiction and how much fact. Some of the pictures included in the book would point readers strongly toward calling it fiction, but there are details in the text itself that go with those which are far too accurate to have merely been guessed at by Luo. The mostly reasonable explanation for this disconnection between the pictures and the text is that one hundred and fifty years had passed since the voyages ceased. And the borders of China, like the section of the archives with information about the fleet, had been sealed for all that time as well. There was no way that the artists could have understood what they were reading, and it was also safer to lean toward to fantastic in their interpretations of what they read.

To that end, the fancifulness of Luo's illustrations can readily be explained by the fact that the emperor in the tale did not make the best choices to retain him a secure grasp on his mandate to rule. And clearly, it never hurts to keep in the good graces the descendants of an emperor who might have lost them their right to rule as well because of his misdeeds … but enough about that for now, it's time to color… and how that all happened has been explained in another book...

"THE ARRIVAL OF ELEPHANTS & RIDERS"

FROM CHAPTER 8

"The Great Ming Nation's Greatest Duty is to its Son of Heaven …

The News of Upcoming Journeys Abroad Merit the Notice of Long-term Visitors"

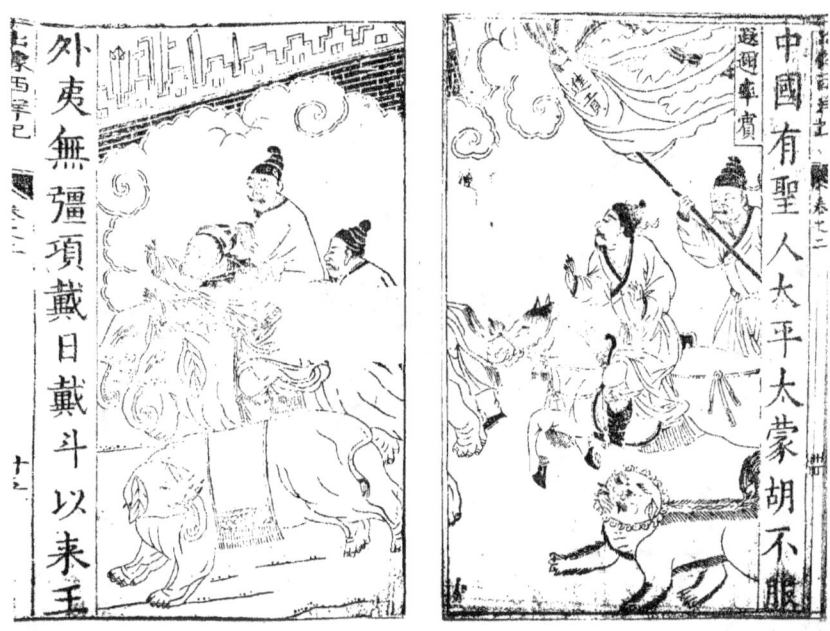

RIGHT CAPTION – 中國有聖人太平太蒙胡服

> In China, there are enlightened Taoist scholars taking their peace & tranquility to the rough barbarian bowmen of the farthest west

RIGHT SMALL – 遐邇率賓

> From far & near, pledges of allegiance are called for

LEFT CAPTION – 外夷無彊項戴日戴斗耒壬

> The foreign barbarians make an effort to show respect to those they contend with

外夷無疆項戴日戴斗以来王

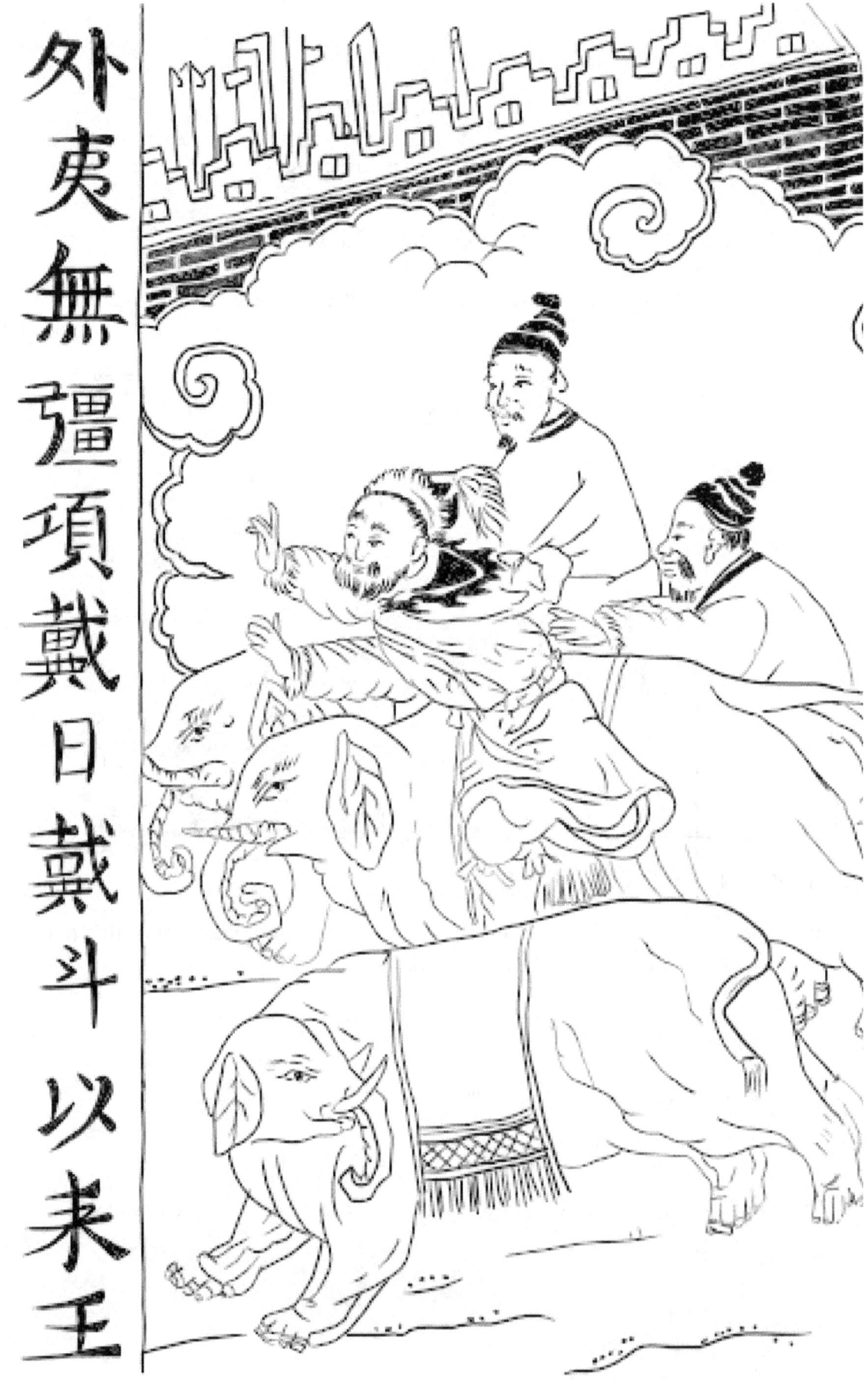

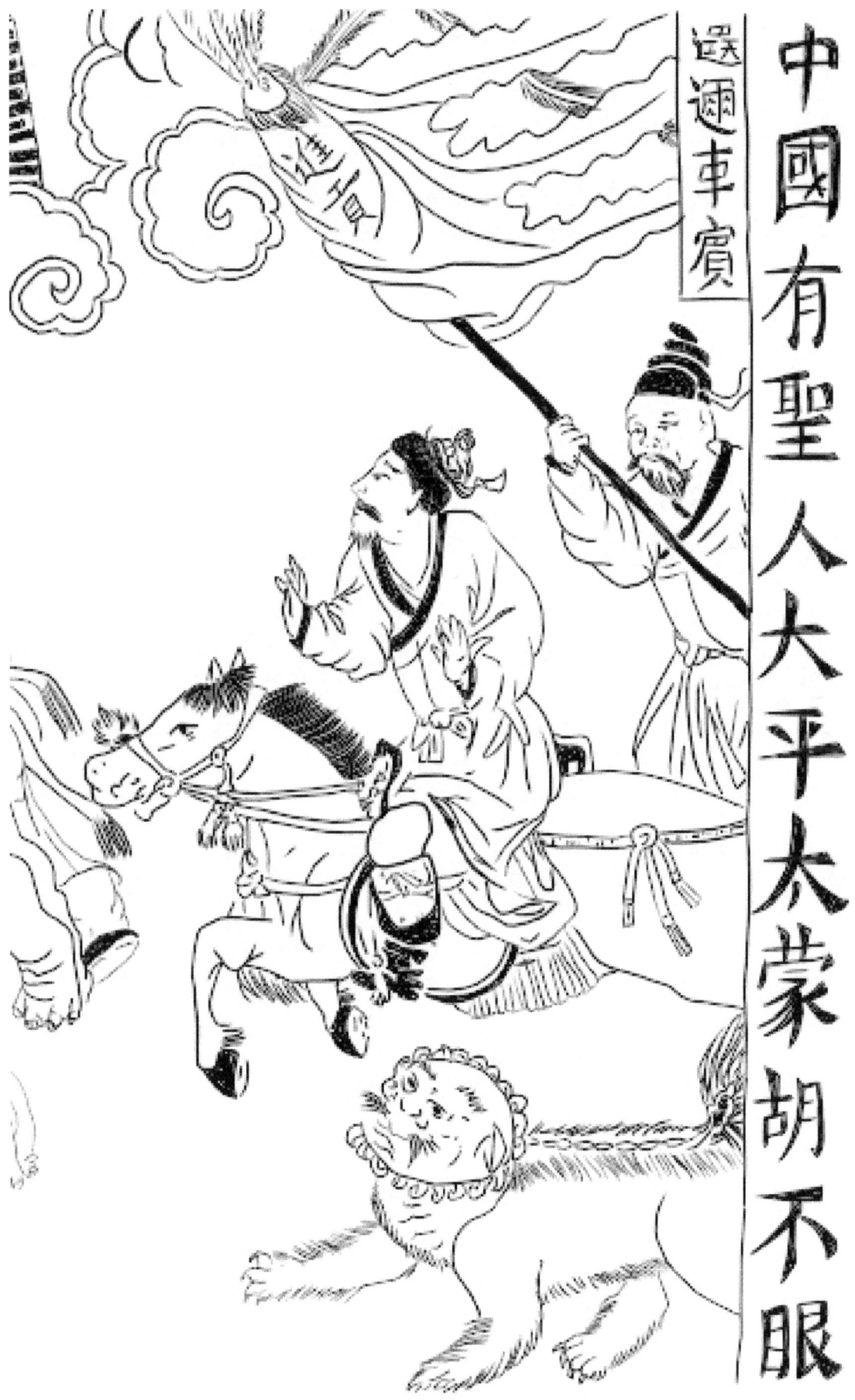

中國有聖人大平太蒙胡不眼

"THE ARMY ADVANCES"

FROM CHAPTER 16

Commanders at the ministry of the army choose the officers who will train the army...

Orders are given for horses to be purchased from markets throughout China

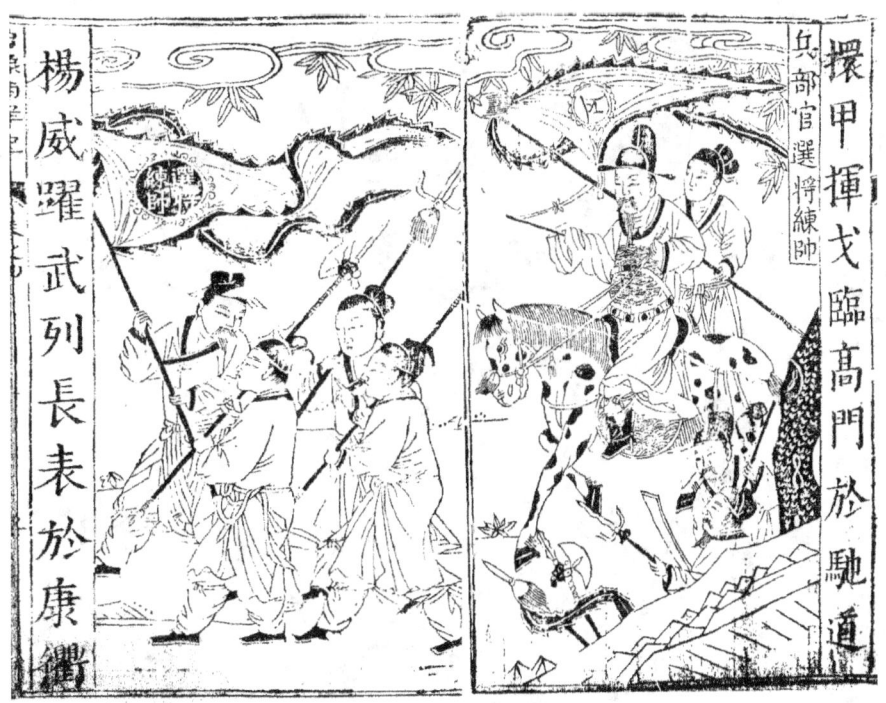

RIGHT CAPTION -- 攌甲揮戈臨高門於馳道

> Upon donning their armor, and just before leaving to march to the battlefield, the troops are eager with regard to being on their way

RIGHT SMALL – 兵部官選将練帥

> The officials of the Ministry of War select and begin to train those of sufficient moral virtue to serve as commanders-in chief

LEFT CAPTION – 楊威躍武列長表於康衢

> Valiant Commander Yang Weiyue constructs his own private list of impressive candidates with regards to the great opportunities ahead of him

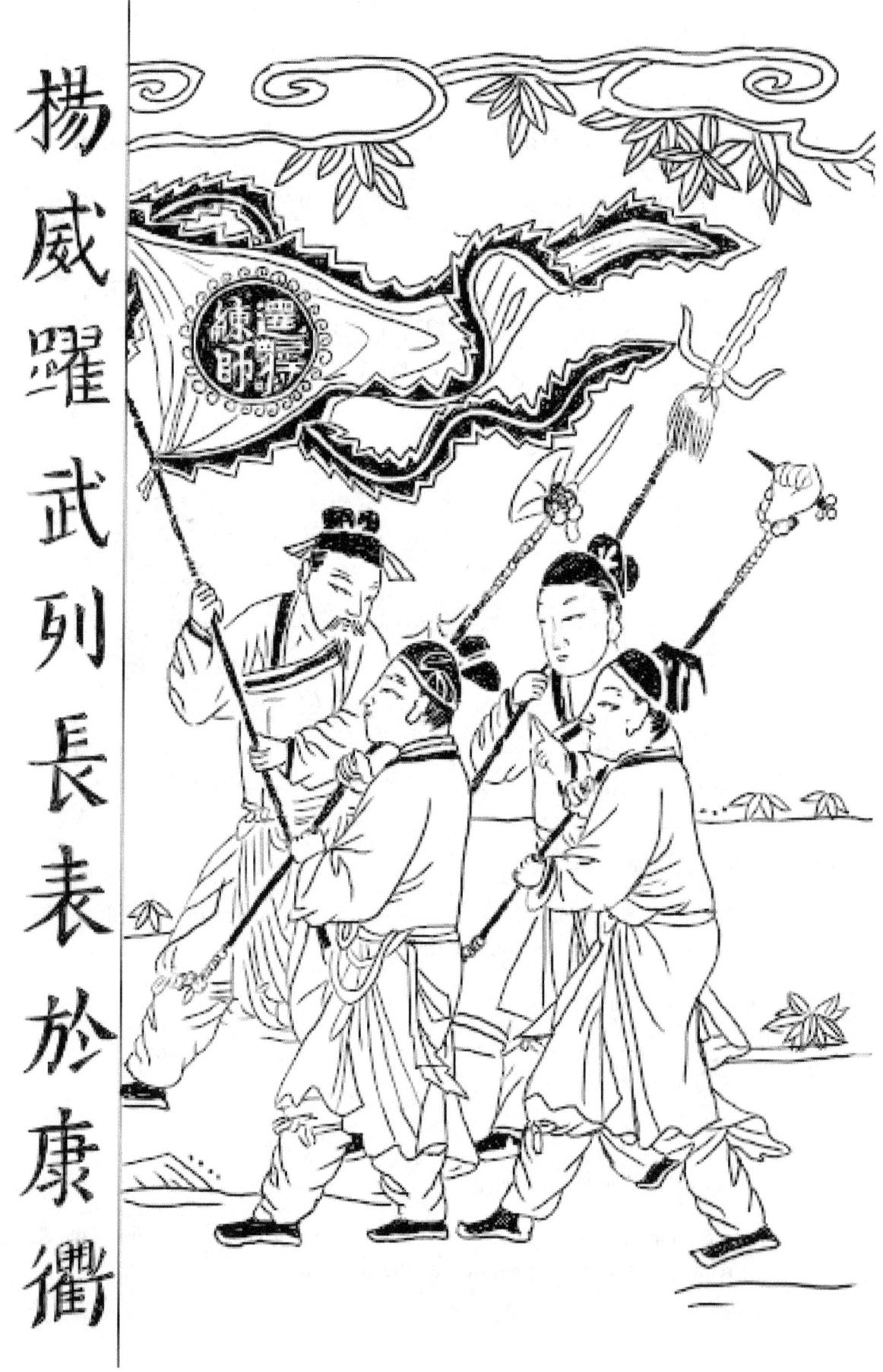

楊威耀武列長表於康衢

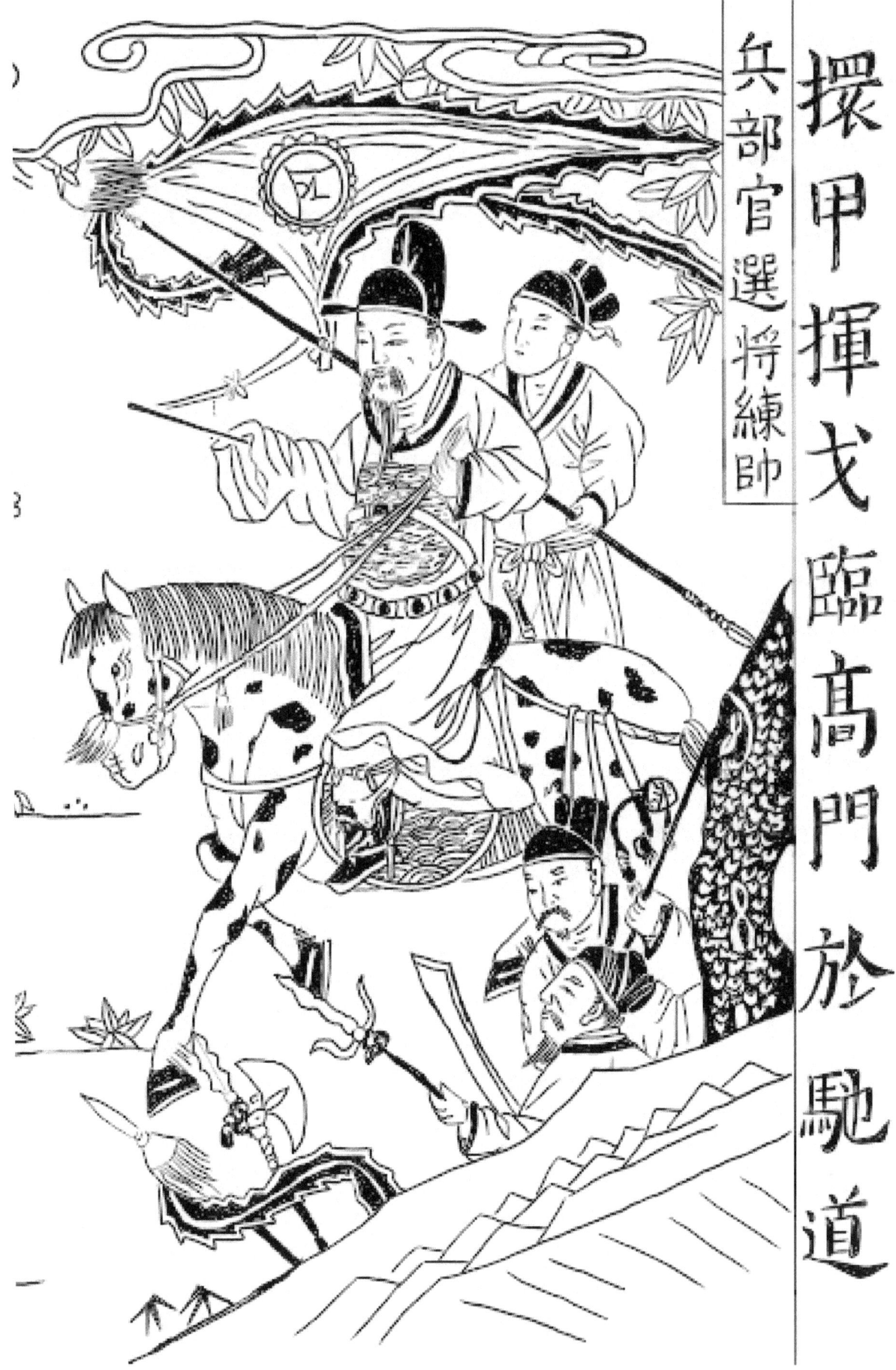

兵部官選將練帥

擐甲揮戈臨高門於馳道

"A CONTENTION BETWEEN LANCERS"

FROM CHAPTER 22

"Because of the Heavenly Queen's Temple, the Gods Send a Lamp to Light the Night …

Before that, a Unit of the Military Contends with Enemies on the Sea of Japan"

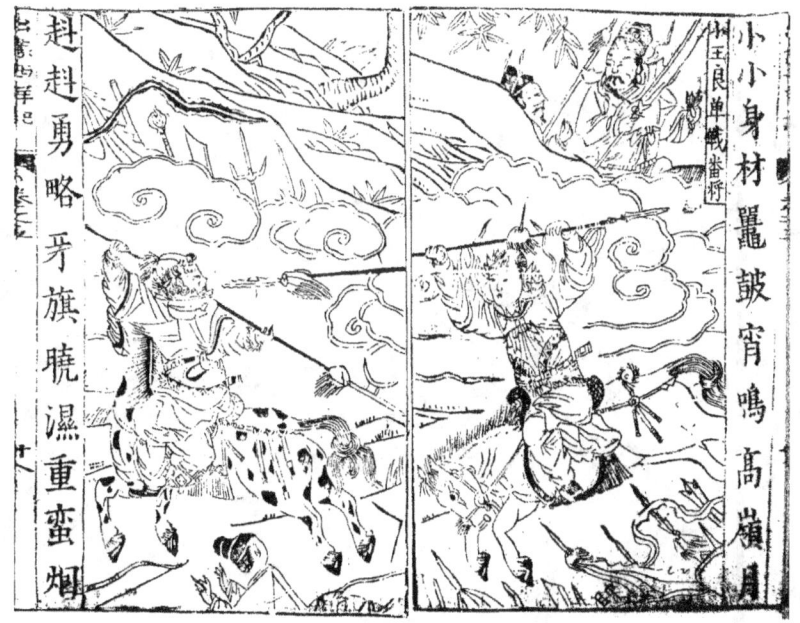

RIGHT CAPTION -- 小小身材鼉皷宵鳴高嶺月

> The small but capable men of the empire of Japan pluck up their courage with the beating of the drum to do battle on their mountains of the Moon

RIGHT SMALL – 小良单戰畨将

> the small but good man does single combat with the foreign general

LEFT CAPTION -- 赳赳勇略牙旗曉濕炮

> All possible wrongs are set right with the seizure of the tooth-edged battle standard of the southern barbarians in the heavy mists of a humid dawn

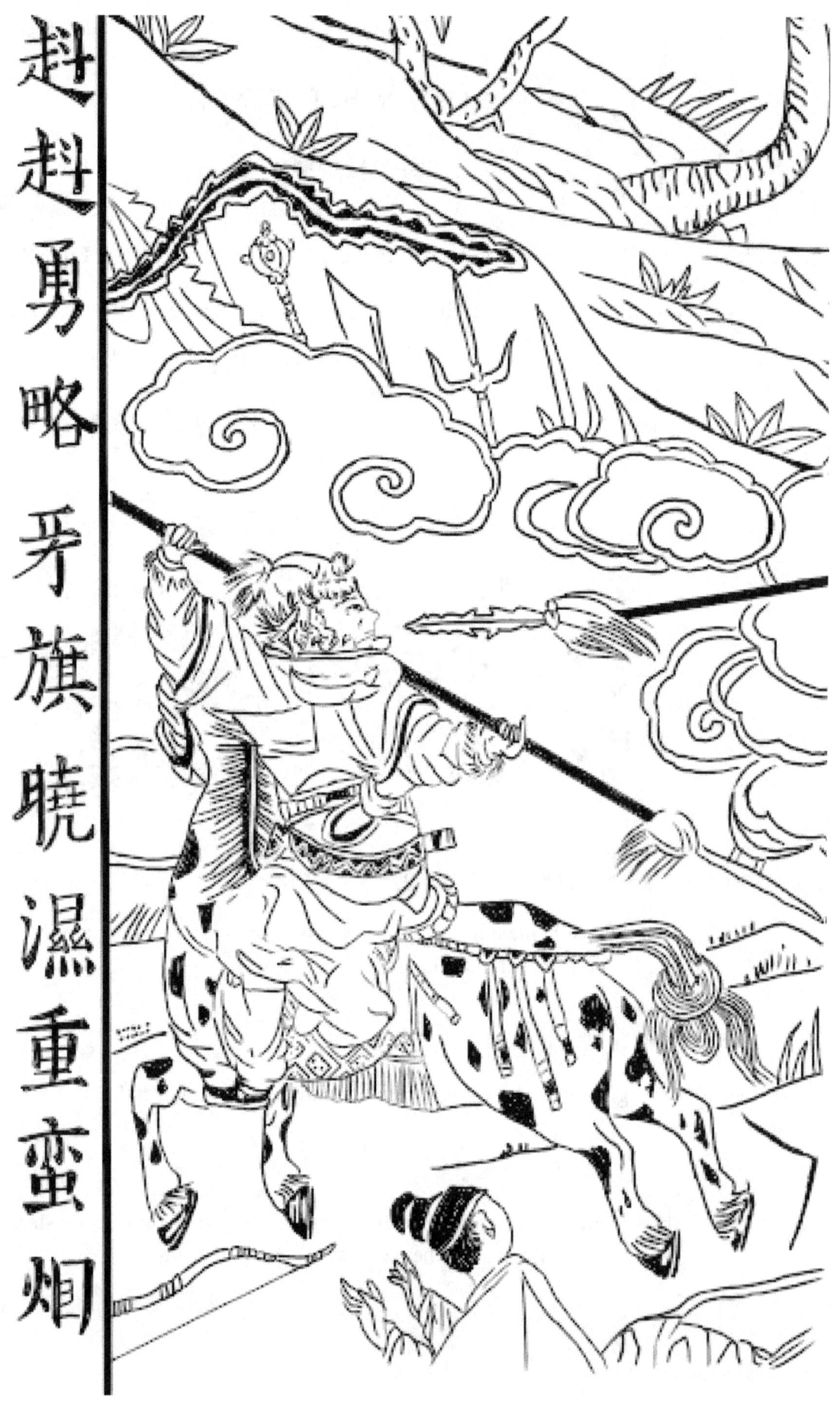

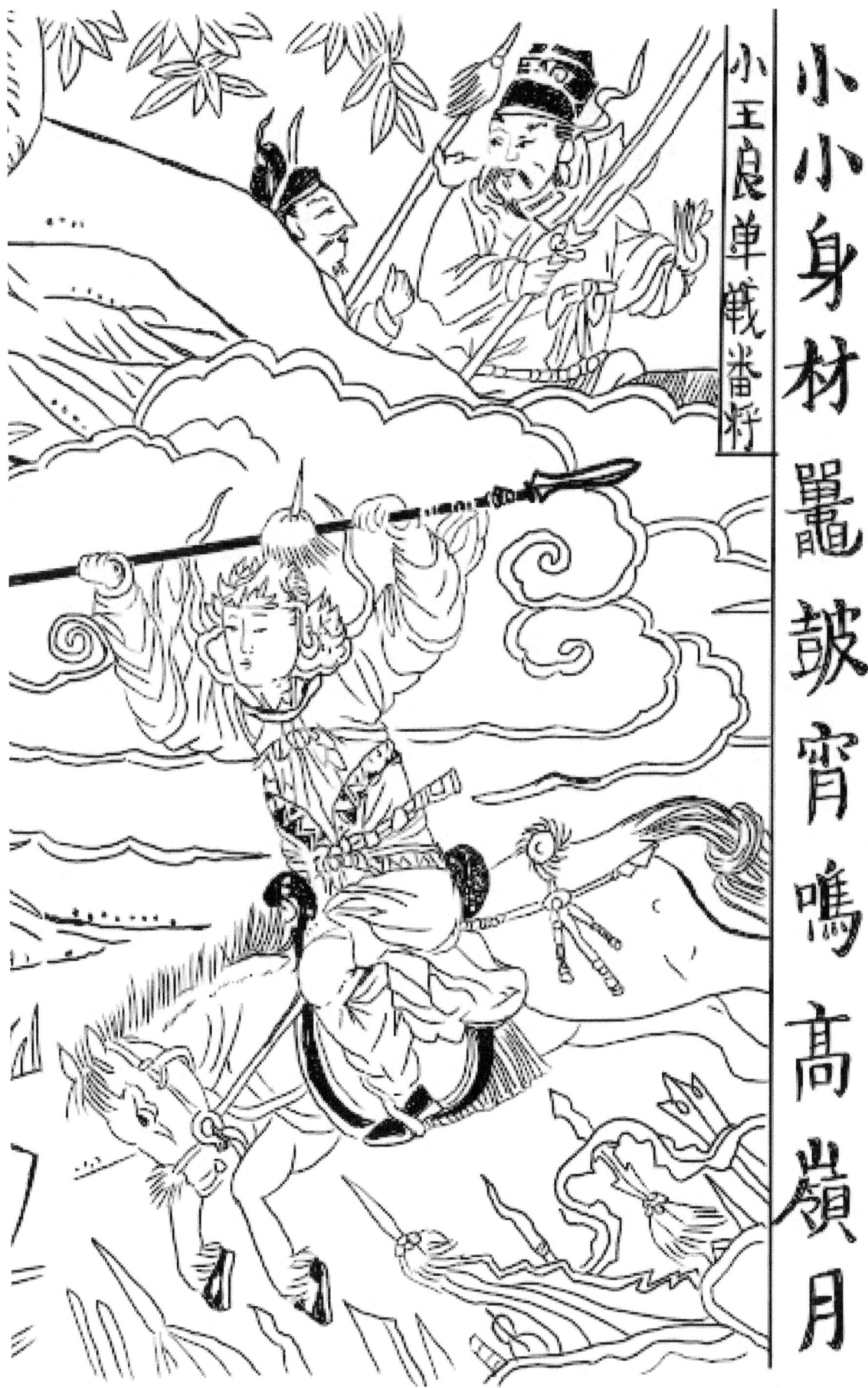

小小身材鼉鼓宵鳴高嶺月

小王良單戰番將

"IN THE FACE OF CONFRONTATION"

FROM CHAPTER 23

A Weak Petty Monarch Trembles
in the Face of Confrontation…

Respected Jiangxin Swiftly Joins the fight,
Slashing with His Magic Sword

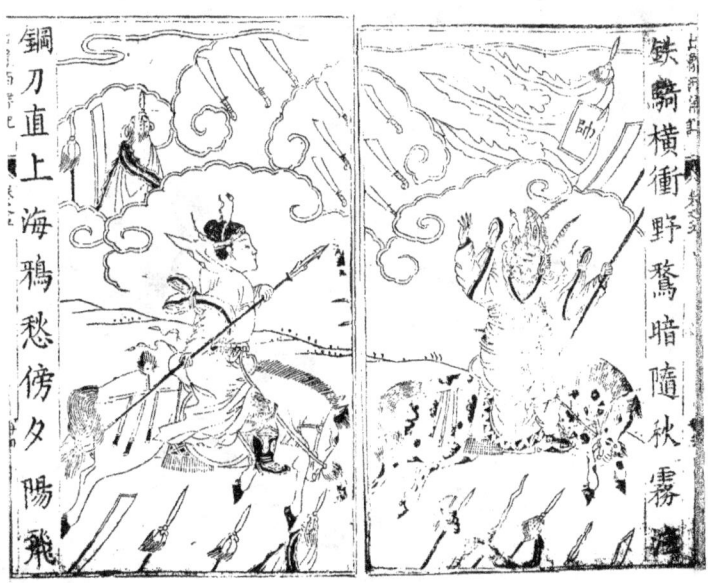

RIGHT CAPTION – 鉄騎橫衝野鶯暗隨秋霧泣

In a wild and violent spearhead of attack, the cavalry goes after what had been a hidden source for a spray of tears

LEFT CAPTION – 鋼刀直上海鴉愁傍夕陽飛

With the tenacity of a steel blade, a great many people are directly moved to gather together to prove a worrisome prophecy of decline is unfounded

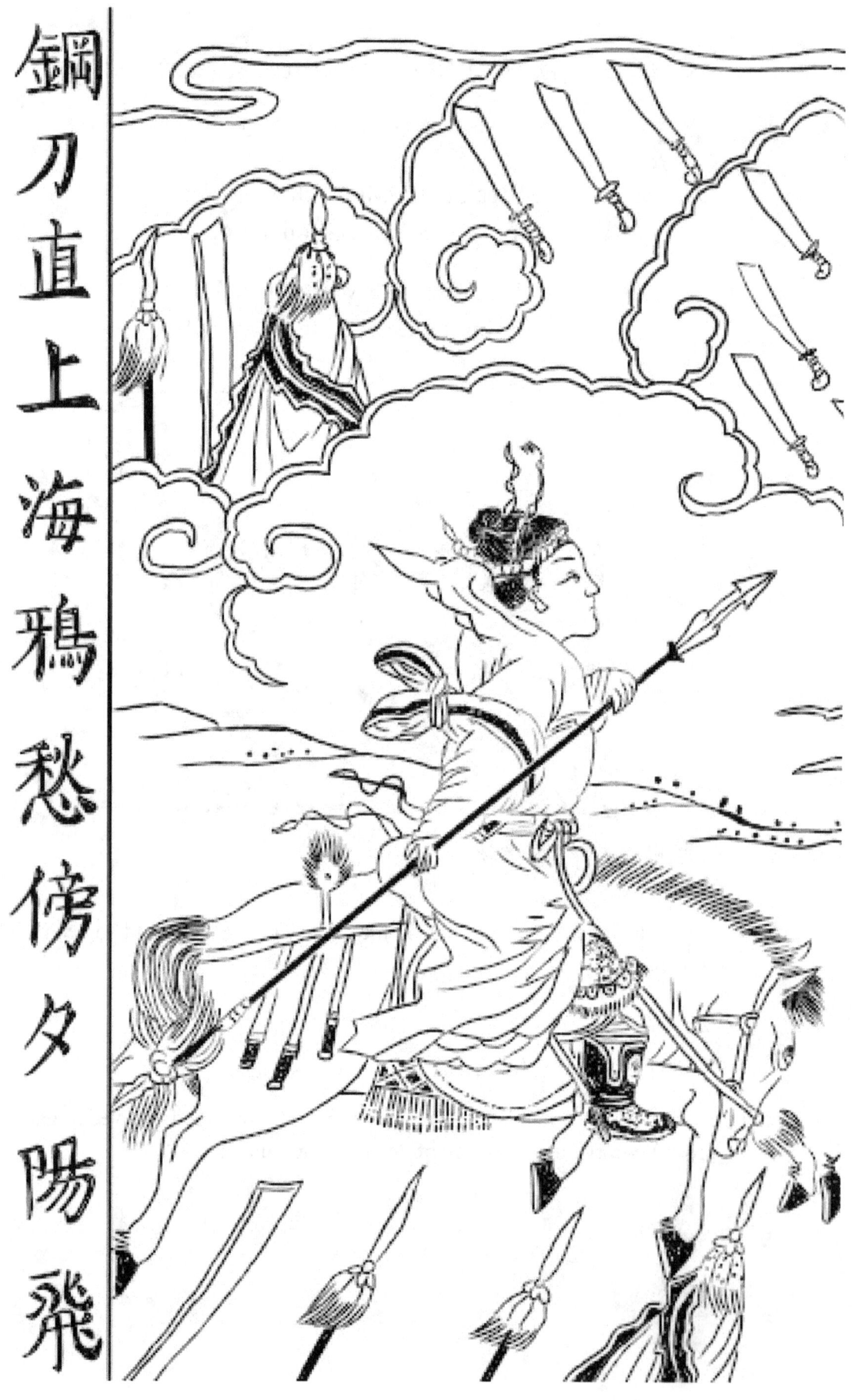

鋼刀直上海鴉愁傍夕陽飛

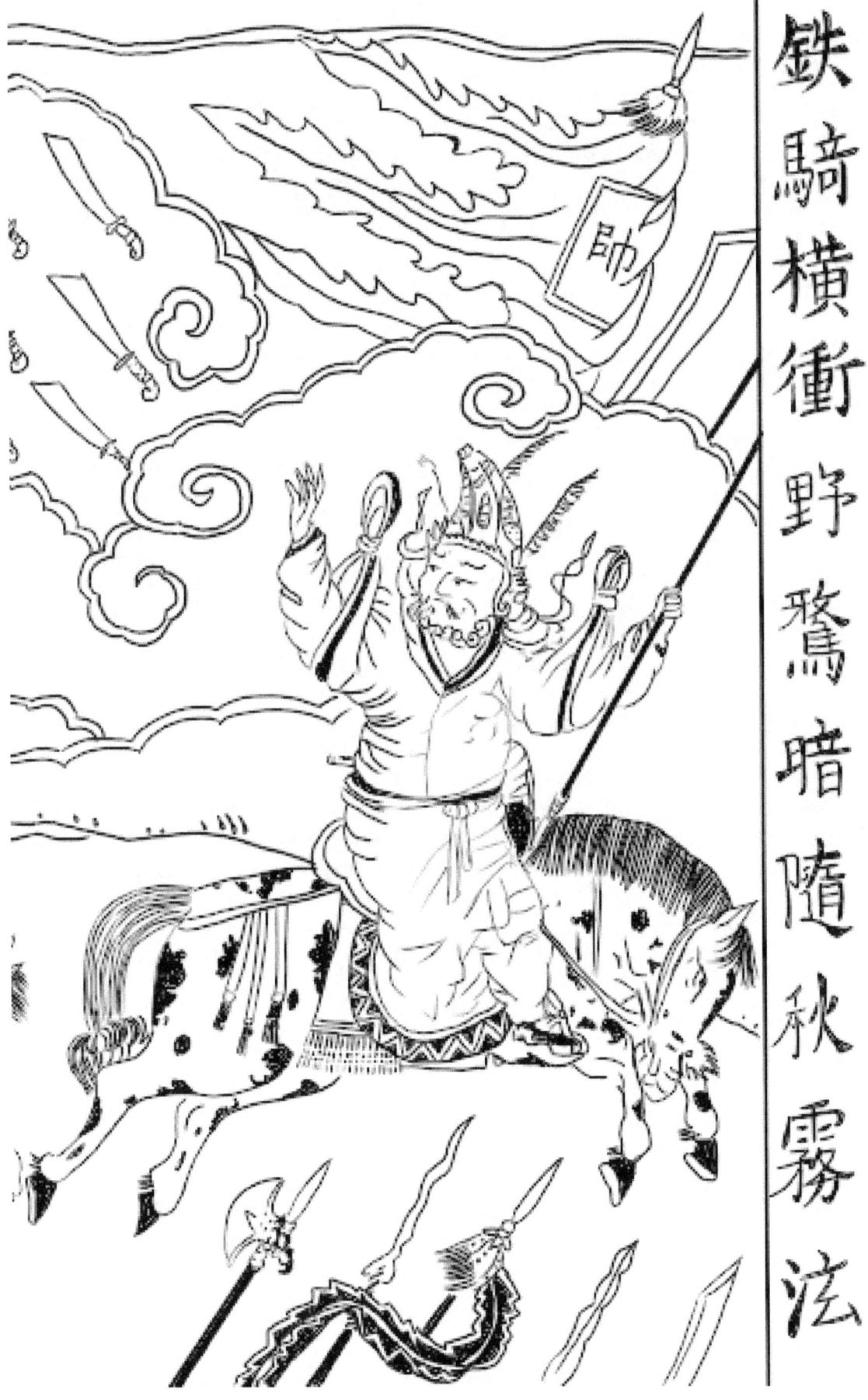

鉄騎橫衝野騖暗隨秋霧泫

帥

"THE FOG AND CONFUSION OF BATTLE"

FROM CHAPTER 24

The premier Chinese scholar alludes to the ill effects of ancient comets...

Jianglin gathers in four commanders from among the flood of applicants

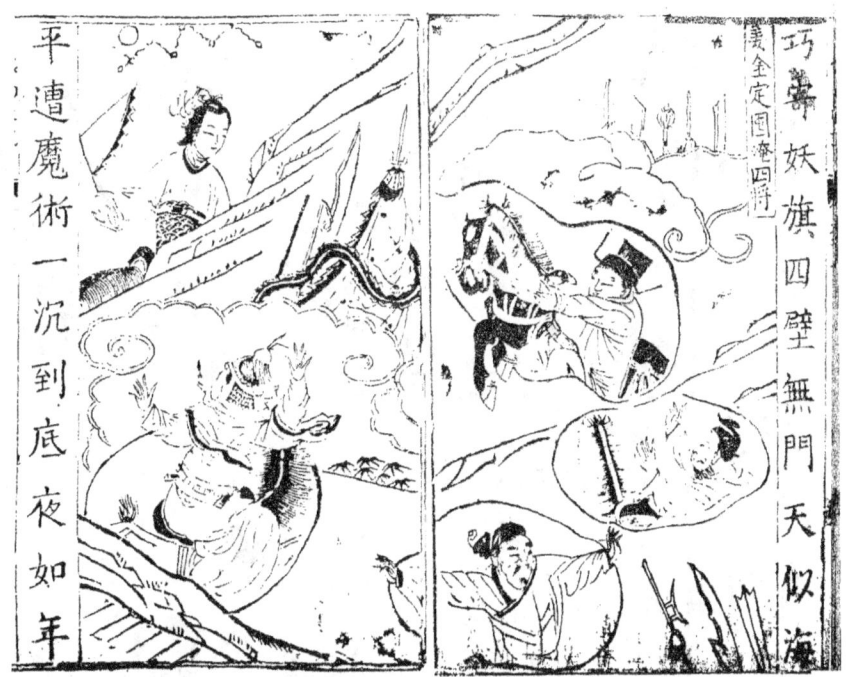

RIGHT CAPTION – 巧寄妖旗四壁無門天似海

> As luck would have it, the utterly demonic folk who had attached themselves to the banner of the four cliffs find out that there is a religious sect that worships far greater deities

RIGHT SMALL – 羑金定囷淹四將

> Propelling matters in a better direction, a flood of gold funds a store of supplies for the four senior generals

LEFT CAPTION -- 遭魔術一沉到底夜如年

> As if by magic, peace is maintained all the way to the night of the end of the New Year's celebrations

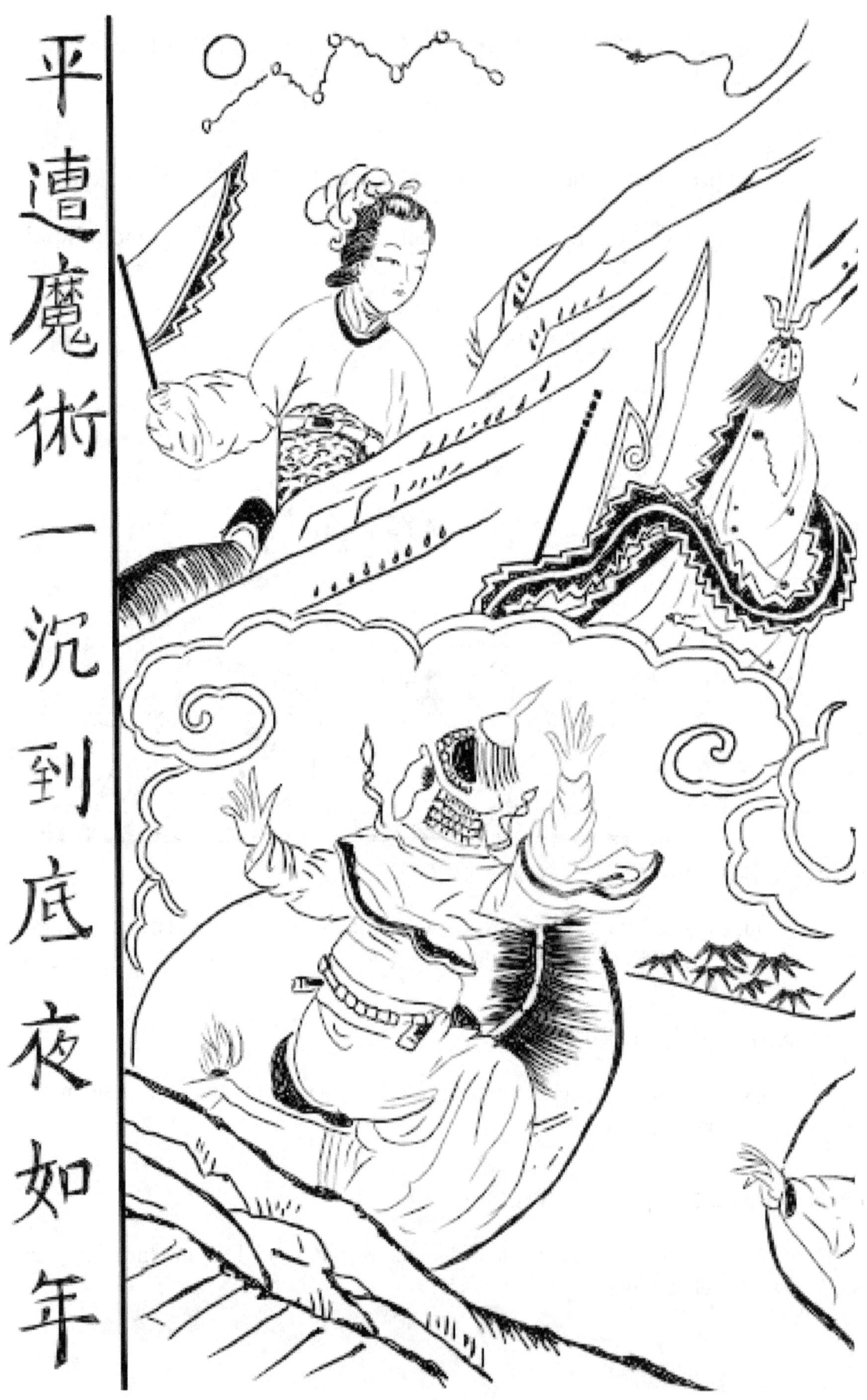

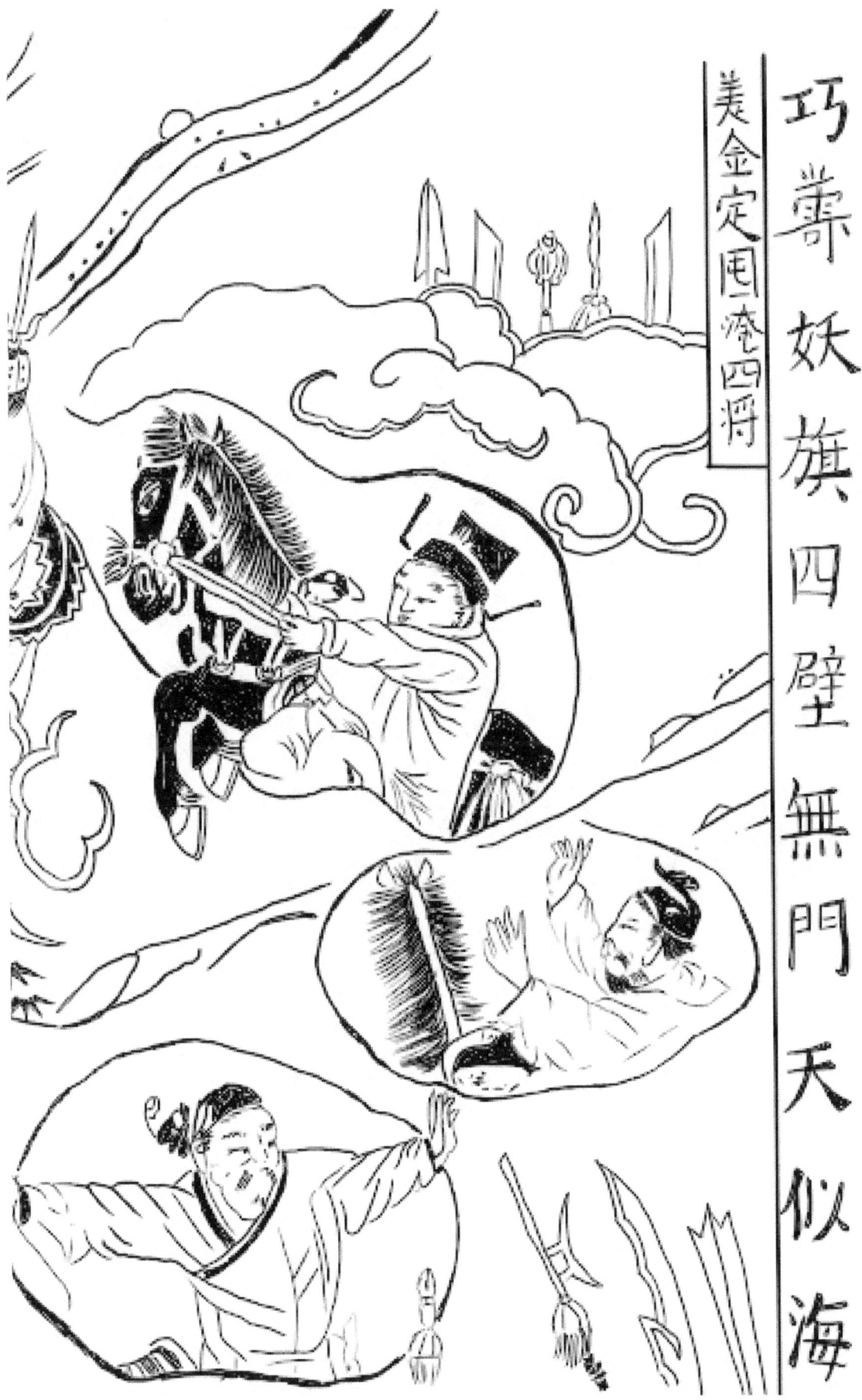

巧誇妖旗四壁無門天似海

羡金定囤淹四將

Laurie Bonner-Nickless

"THE FOUR COMMANDERS COME TOGETHER"

FROM CHAPTER 24

The premier Chinese scholar alludes to the ill effects of ancient comets...

Jiangjin gathers four commanders from among the flood of applicants

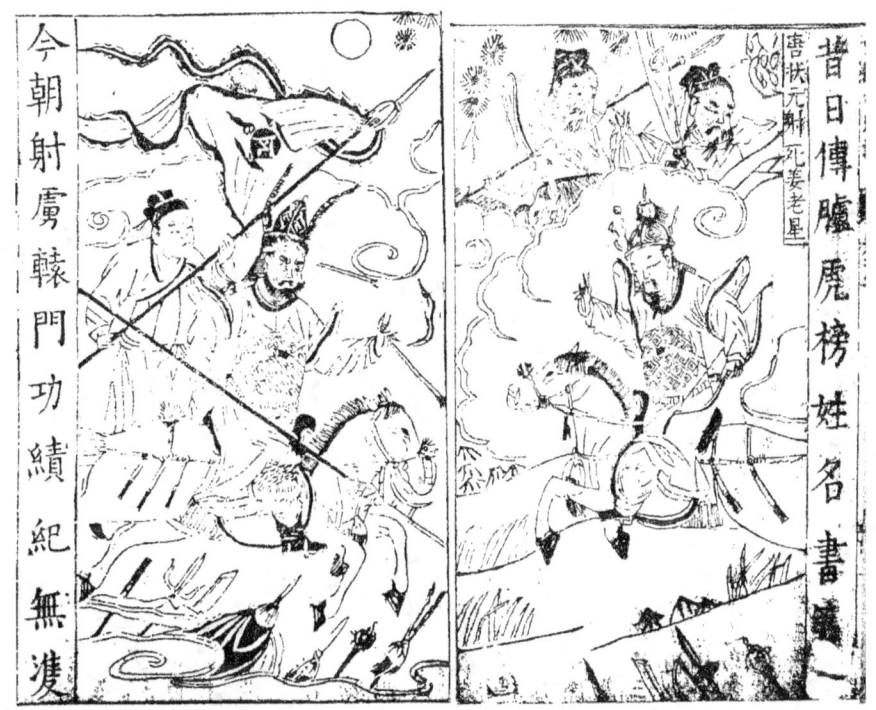

RIGHT CAPTION – 昔日傳臚虎榜姓各書第一

> In former times, the great histories began by listing rosters of heroes one and all in order by each of their family names

RIGHT SMALL – 唐状元射死羑老星

The pre-eminent chinese scholar alludes to that the direction of the north star is fixed in its place

LEFT CAPTION -- 令朝射虜轅門功績紀無雙

> There is no record of meritorious deeds that includes an Imperial order to shoot prisoners at the city gate

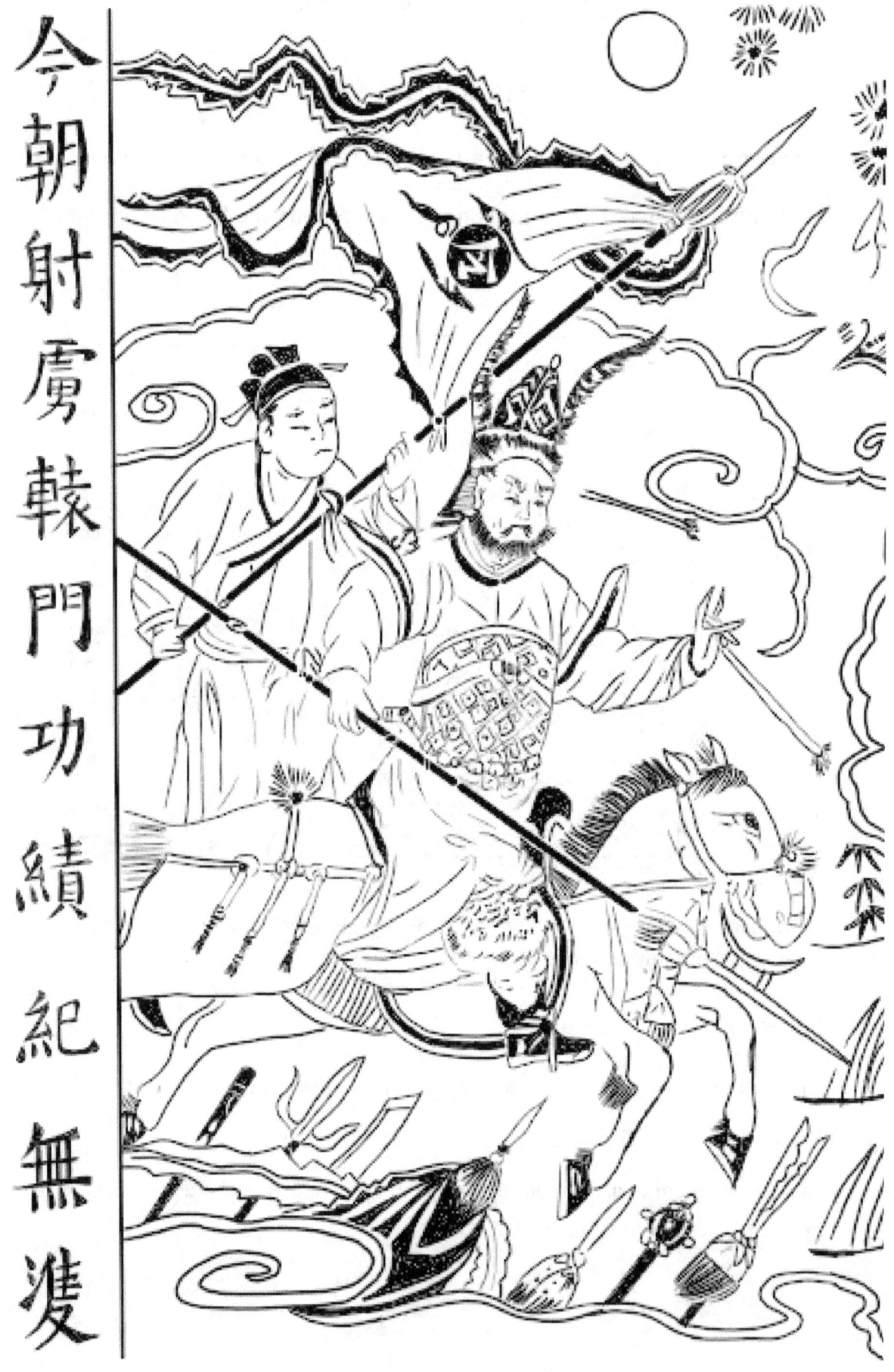

今朝射虜轅門功績紀無渡

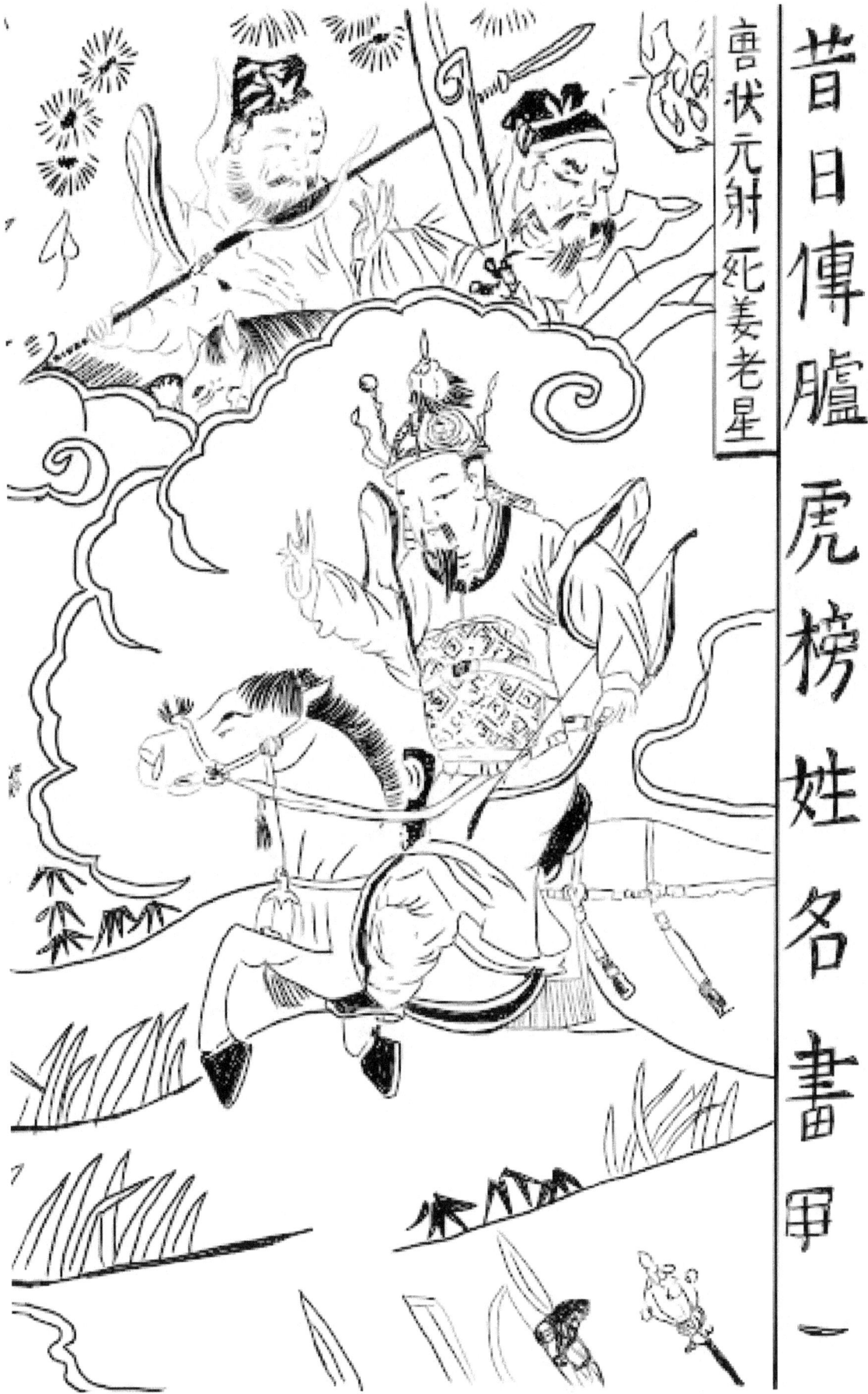

昔日傳臚虎榜姓名書甲一

唐伏元射死姜老星

"CONCERN FOR THE FALLEN LADY"

FROM CHAPTER 25

The Taoist Master plots how to seize control of

those subscribing to the powers of Venus...

Jianglin orders gathering up those who have evaded forced conscription

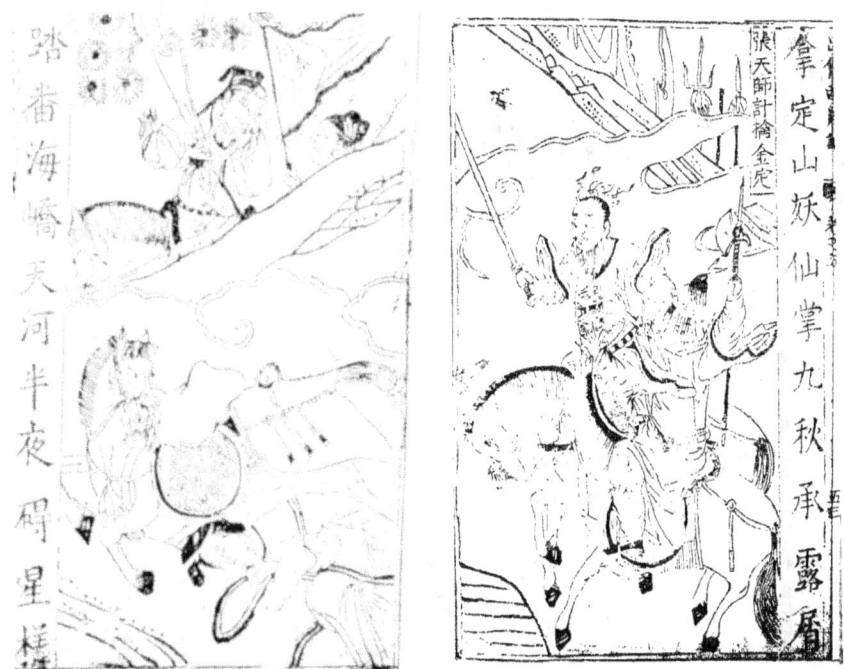

RIGHT CAPTION – 拿定山妖仙掌九秋承露屑

The decision is made in the ninth month atop Huashan Peak stoop to accepting manna

RIGHT SMALL – 張天師討檄金定

The supreme leader of the Taoist sect sharply criticizes Jieqin about decisions that had been thought settled about Venus

LEFT CAPTION – 踏番海嶠天河半夜碍星槎

Upon going to the place where the great number of foreigners are gathered on the mountains by the sea, it is noticed that a new heavenly body has appeared to obscure the Milky Way

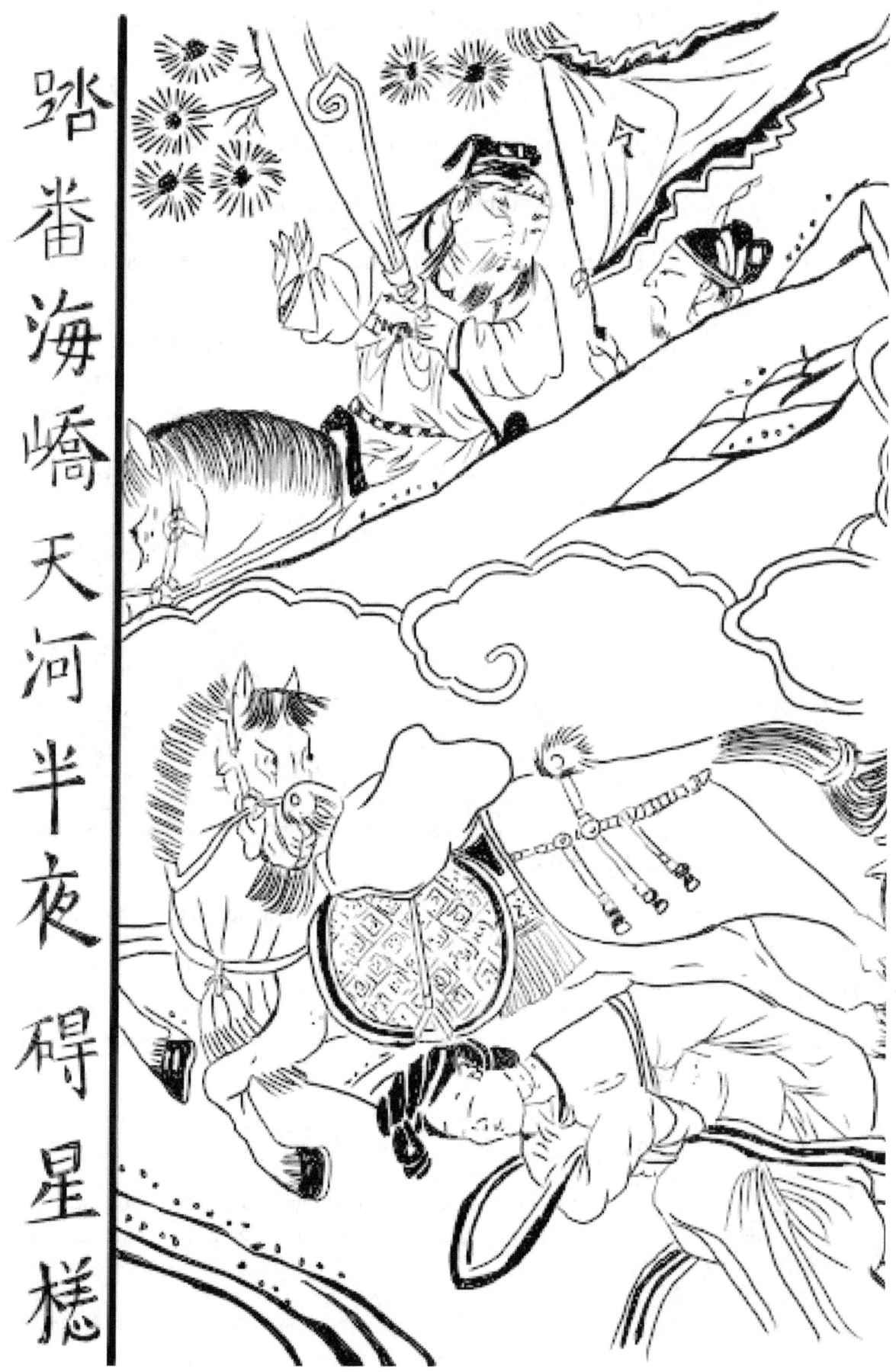

踏番海嶠天河半夜碍星樣

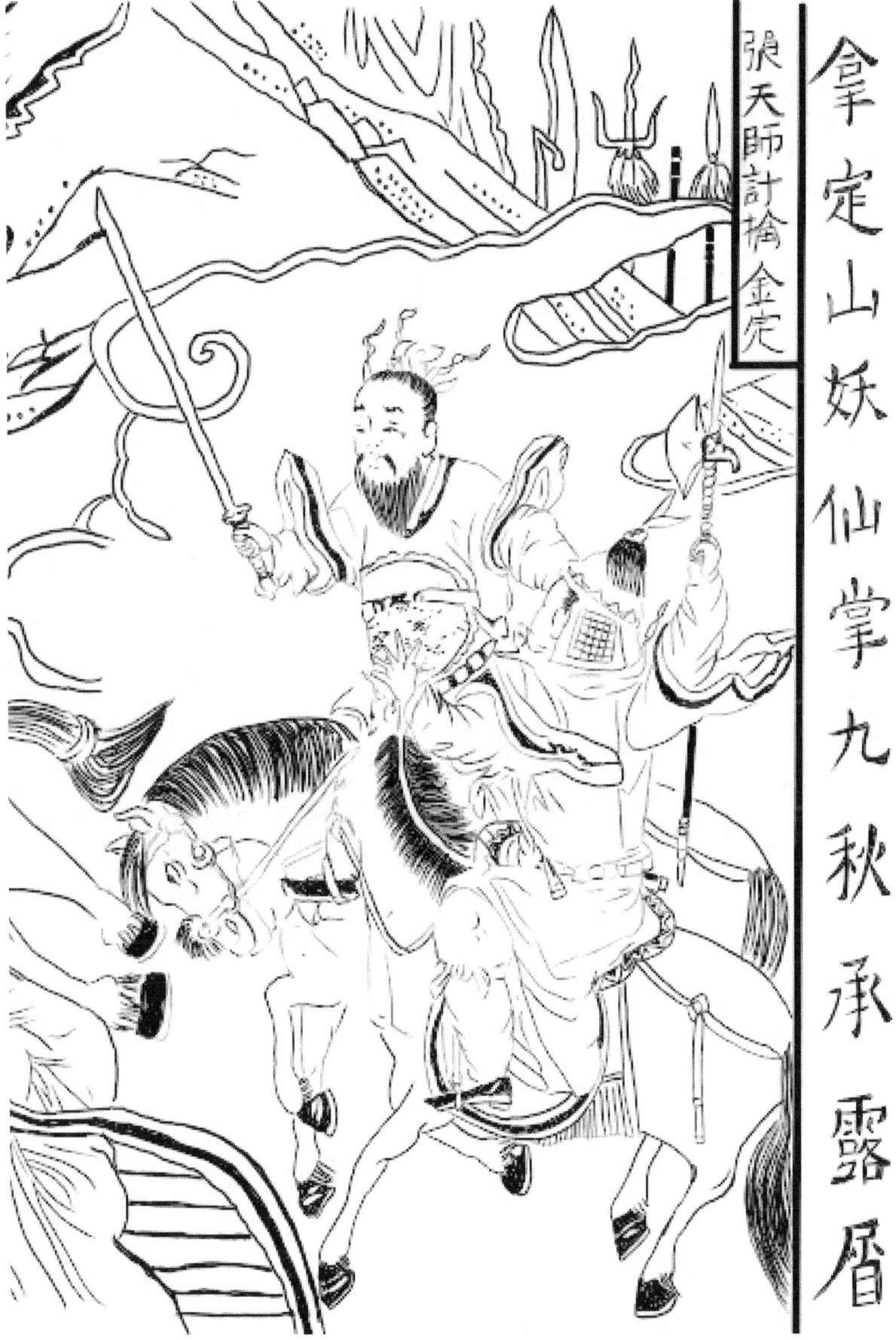

拿定山妖仙掌九秋承露屑

張天師討擒金定

"A WIDE ASSORTMENT OF COMMANDERS RIDE TO BATTLE"

FROM CHAPTER 27

Different military commanders both ponder joining the expedition ...

The Taoist Master sets out with three great military commanders

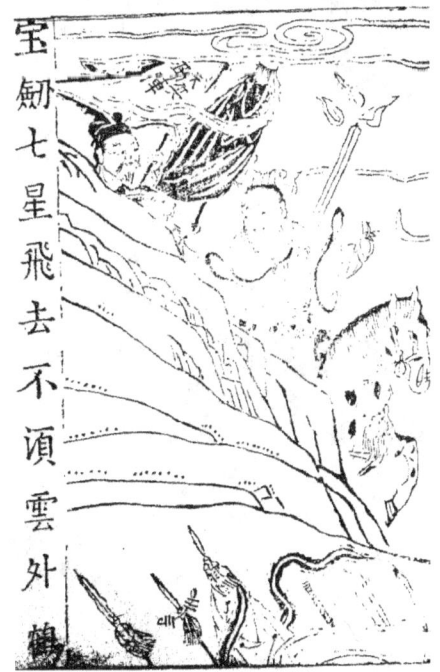 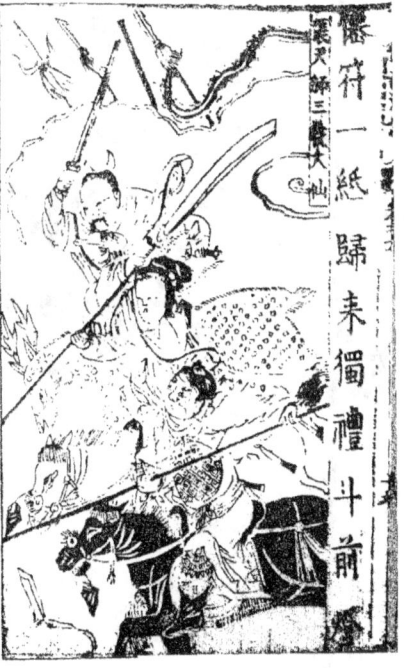

RIGHT CAPTION – 僊符紙歸采獨禮斗前燈

>The Taoist immortal submits to a written agreement to surrender the authority of command to another only because of the new body in the heavens

RIGHT SMALL – 張天師戰大仙

>The senior Taoist master contends with another Taoist immortal

LEFT CAPTION -- 宝劍七星飛去不頃雲外鶴

>The sword of seven stars is given into the keeping of one who will be far from the reach of those to whom he owes his filial piety for a long time

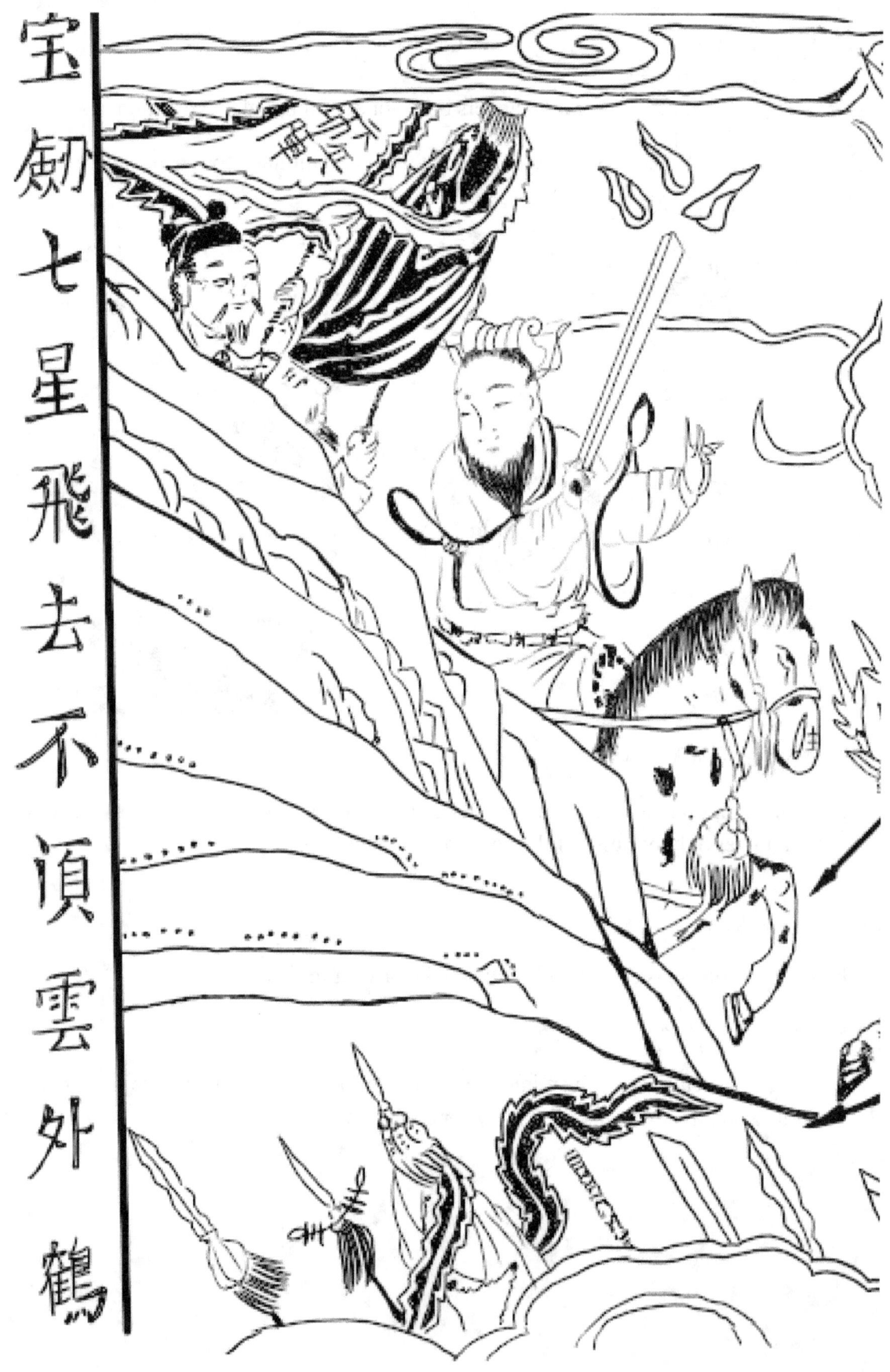

宝劍七星飛去不頂雲外鶴

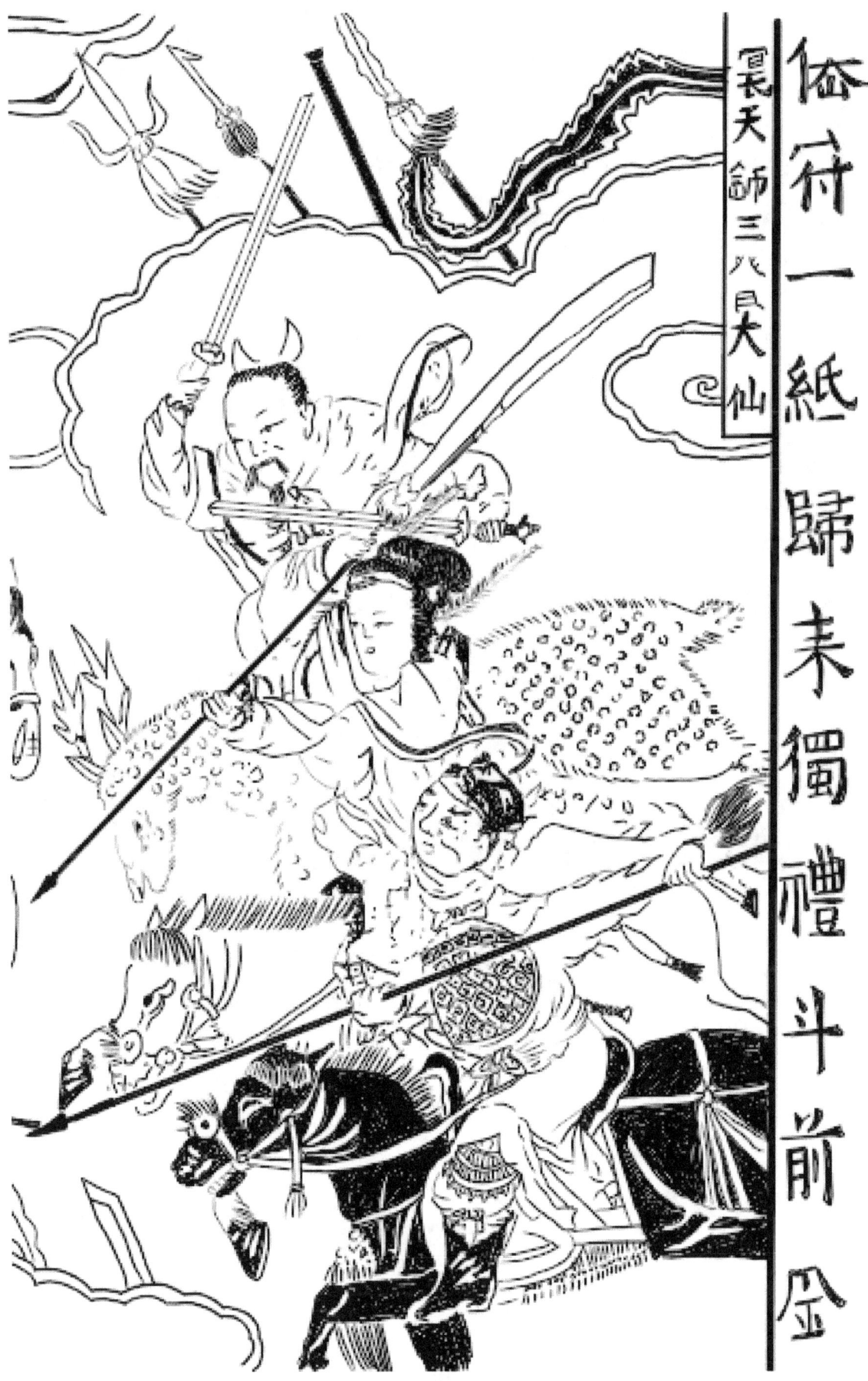

俵符一紙歸未獨禮斗前盆

冒長天師三八員天仙

"AN ARCHER & A LANCER CONTEND BEFORE THE CITY WALLS"

FROM CHAPTER 31

Jianglin plots to carry out three most clever ruses...

The very young imperial monarch offers gifts of funds

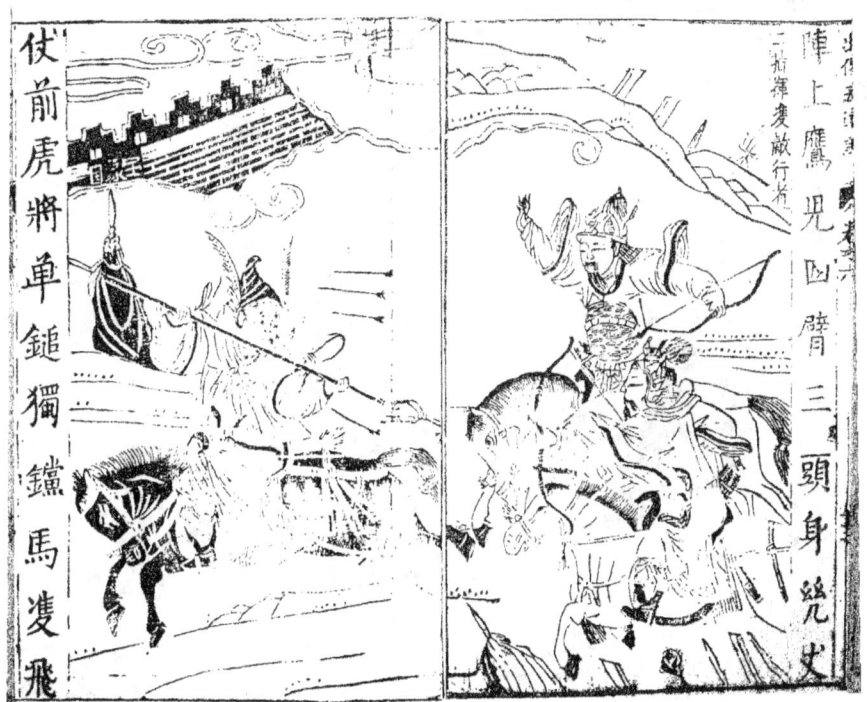

RIGHT CAPTION – 陣上鷹児四臂三頭身絟丈

The truly visionary battle plans of the four young eagles (courageous commanders) leads to the first taking up of arms by the men of the garrisons connected to them

RIGHT SMALL – 二措揮薆敵行者

Two sets of plans are made: one, to send out an attacking army; two, to send out wandering missionary monks

LEFT CAPTION -- 仗虎將鎚獨鑞馬薆飛

Before the battle begins, the four commanders make plans for the cavalry's arming, and for it to be ready to fly

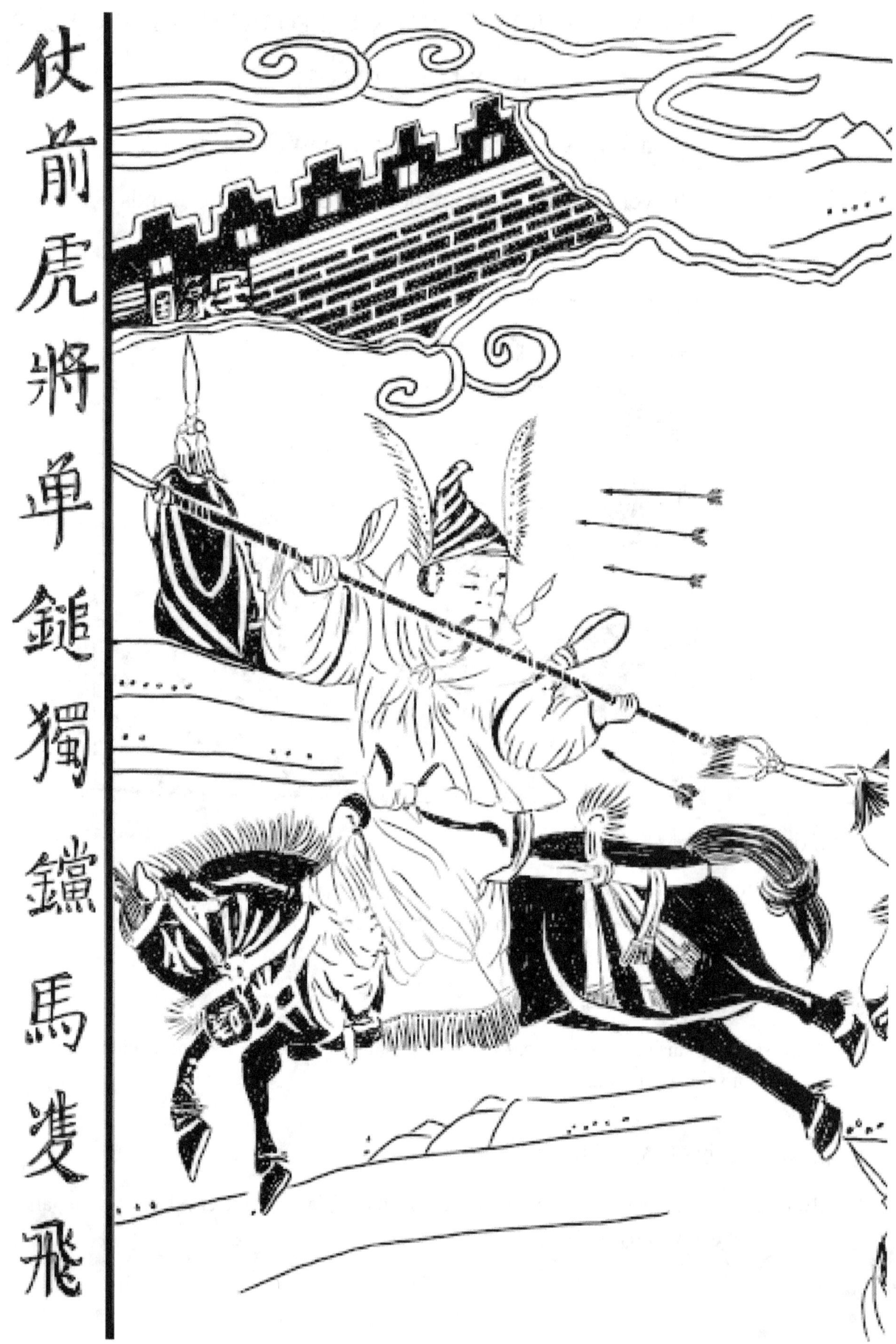

仗前虎將單鎚獨鐋馬雙飛

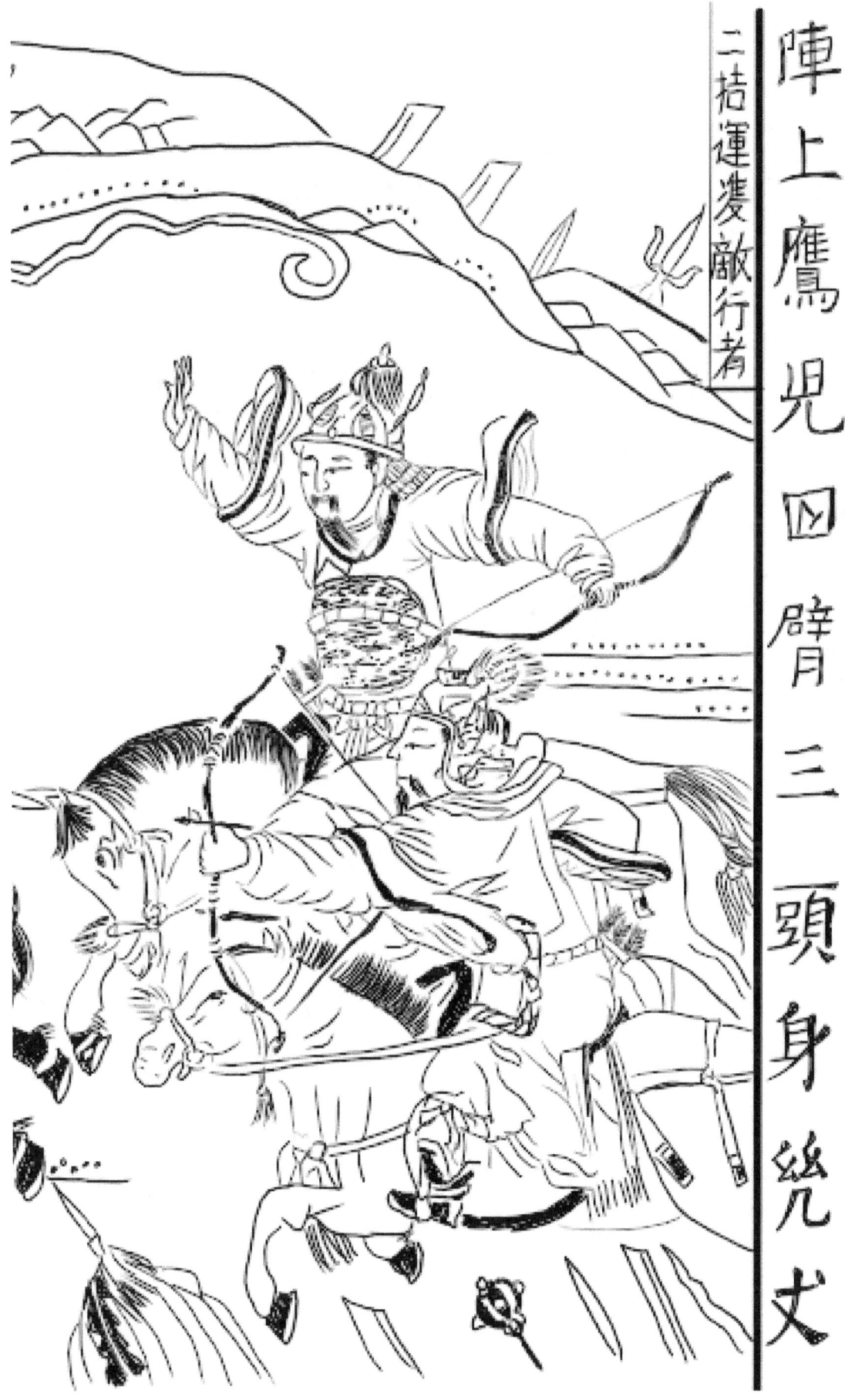

陣上鷹兒囮臂三頭身綻戈

二桔運逢敵行者

"ADVANCING BOTH INTO BATTLE AND INTO LEGENDS"

FROM CHAPTER 31

Jianglin plots to carry out three most clever ruses...

The very young imperial monarch offers gifts of funds

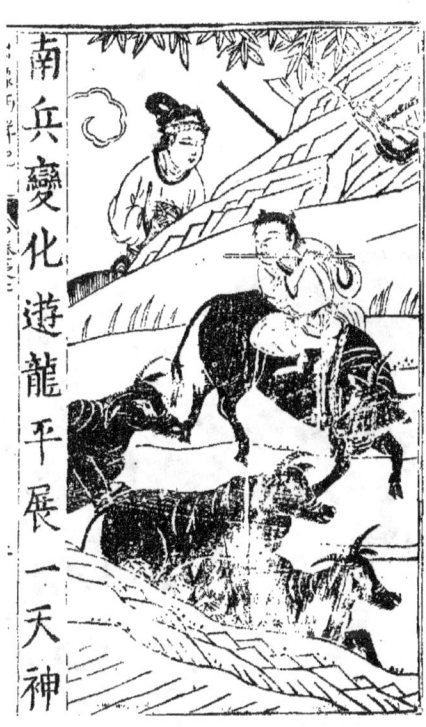 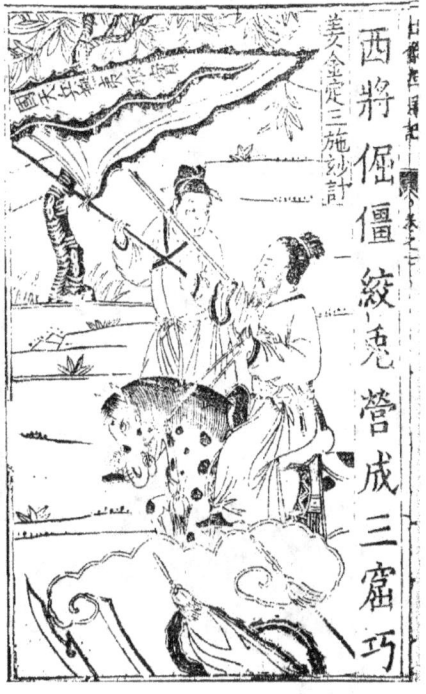

RIGHT CAPTION – 西將倔僵絞兔營成三窟巧

The surly commander-in-chief for the west is deadlocked by long-term entanglements within the senior-most barracks that luckily turn out to also be the den of fortuitous opportunities

RIGHT SMALL -- 姜金定施紗計

Golden Ginger is put to use in an ingenious strategy

LEFT CAPTION – 南兵變化遊龍平展一天神

In the South, the military strategy for those who will be wandering on the behalf of the Emperor is to spread everywhere abroad a belief in the celestial gads

南兵變化遊龍平展一天神

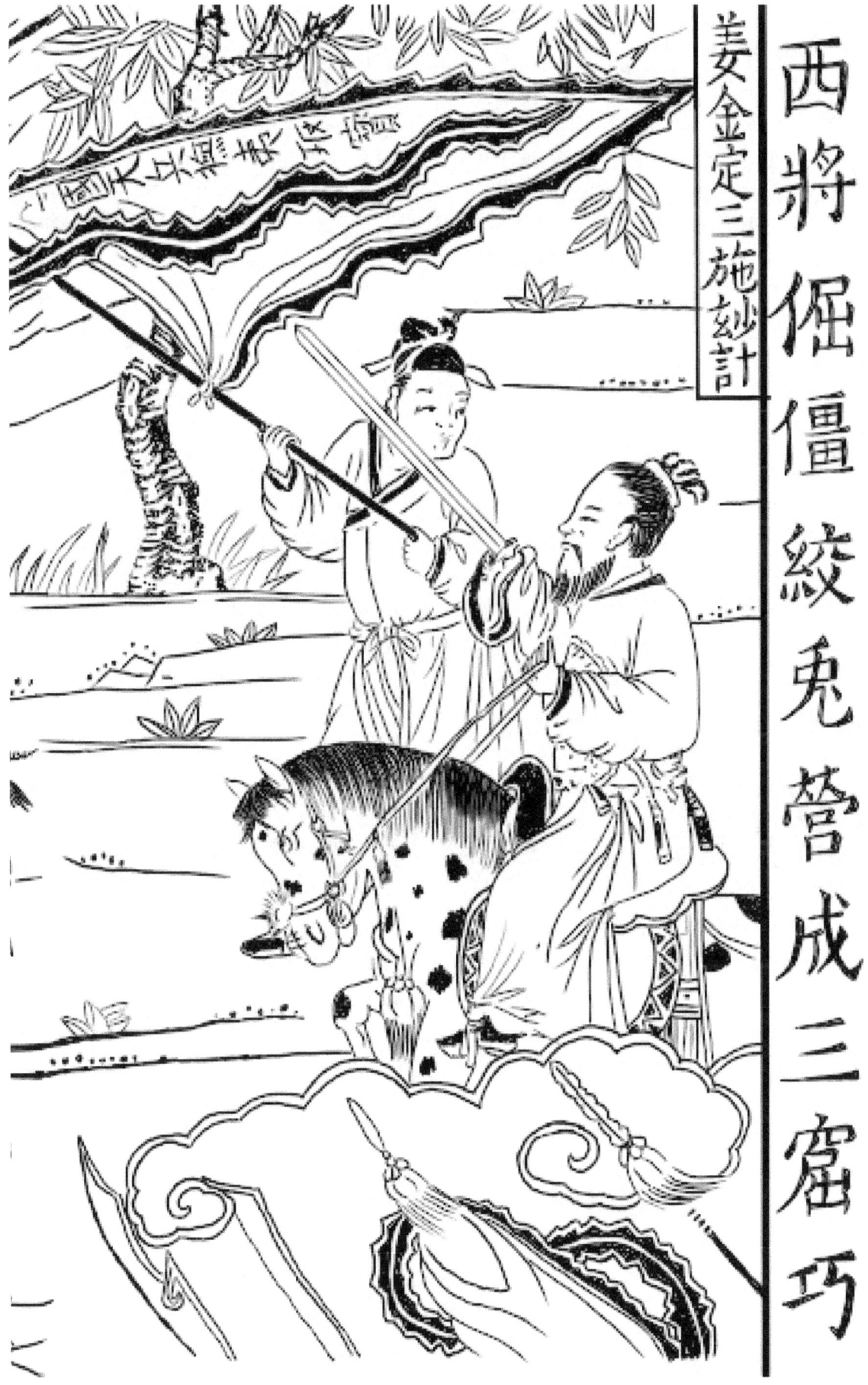

西將倔僵絞兔營成三窟巧

姜金定三施玅計

51

ABOUT THE RESTORER-TRANSLATOR

I grew up on and around United States Air Force Bases around the USA, but mostly west of the Mississippi. I got my college degrees in film making, and television production. Since 2006, I have been working on translating the Luo epic story of the final voyages of the great Ming Treasure Fleet. I am currently a member of the Silk Road Sustainable Development Institute's Experts Panel for my work as a translator & research historian, the content of which has been verified by language & history scholars in Asia, as well by the director emeritus of the Library of Congress' Asian division. My other books include a work of fiction titled A World, A Yonder, and two nonfiction books -- Chasing Dragons, the True history of the Piasa, and To the Gates of Fengtu. The lattermost book being the translation of the final 15 chapters of Luo's epic tale.

I currently live in Missouri, with my husband & research partner, Mark, two cats who think that I work for them, and the younger of my two daughters, in a small house not too far from the Mississippi River, and several other sites which figure prominently in Luo's epic account of Chinese explorers in pre-Columbian North America.

For other books by this author, see:

A World, A Yonder as L. L. Bonner, a fantasy novel.

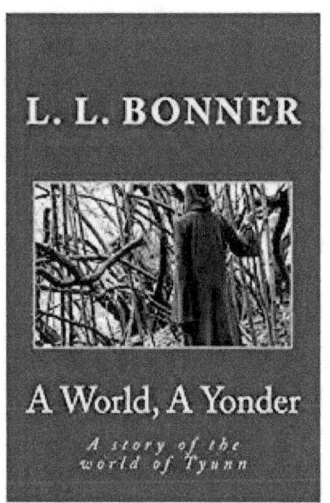

Chasing Dragons, the true history of the Piasa, Expanded Edition with Mark Nickless. A non-fiction examination of a lost local landmark, what it really looked like, the real reasons behind its destruction, and the body of evidence to prove it's origins are connected to an unexpected source in 1433.

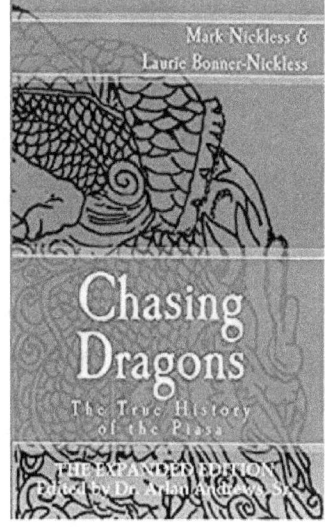

To the Gates of Fengtu, the first modern translation of the final 15 chapters of an account of the seventh and final set of voyages of the Ming Treasure Fleet, and it's commander, Zheng He, the real man behind the legends of Sinbad.

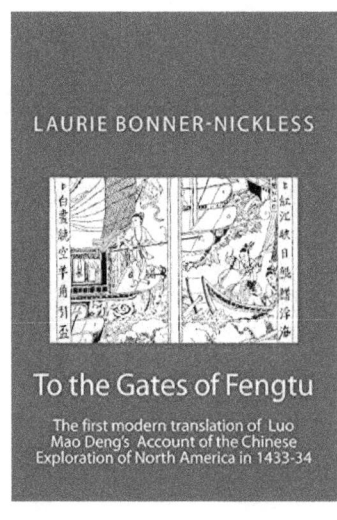

www.ingramcontent.com/pod-product-compliance
Lightning Source LLC
Chambersburg PA
CBHW080912220526
45467CB00021BA/3287